MW01698109

To Frank,

A video on the subject of this book is available in DVD format at www.budointernational.com

© Of this edition. Budo International Publ. Co.
All the studio photographs are the work of Alfredo Tucci.

All rights reserved for the Spanish language edition and for any another. The total or partial reproduction in any way, written or spoken, or by any means, magnetic or electronic, without the authorization of the publishing company or both authors is forbidden.

Graphic production: SERGRAPH, S.L.
ISBN: 978-84-92484-15-7
Legal deposit: M-54428-2008

BUDO INTERNATIONAL
CINTURON NEGRO
CINTURÃO NEGRO
BLACKBELT UK
KAMPFKUNST INTERNATIONAL
BUDO INTERNATIONAL
BUDO INTERNATIONAL

Team of Poomsae & Technique European and World Champions

Taekwondo Poomsaes

Advanced Poomsae 9-17

FEDERACIÓN ESPAÑOLA DE TAEKWONDO

Index

Preface

After the previous book, "Basic Poomsaes", and its superb editing, I am pleased to present, even with more enthusiasm, this second work on the High Poomsae of Taekwondo.

The excellent graphics quality, design and layout give a proper perspective and show our Sport and Martial Art as we all in the great family of Taekwondo wish it to be finally perceived by society. That is why we are confident that the translation of this work into six languages will provide all members of the great family of Taekwondo in the world a valuable tool for the proper spreading of this unique Martial art and Olympic sport.

Similarly, we are all pleased in the Federation with the DVD on High Poomsae, a work which is especially complementary to this book and which had preceded it in time. Together, they form a unique example of practical handbooks in terms of teaching and learning the ways of Taekwondo in the world.

Both works are official documents of the Spanish Federation of Taekwondo. Later, they will be presented and offered for acceptance as reference texts for other Federations, both in Europe and Latin America.

However, any student within the World Federation will find a guide at the highest level, regardless of his latitude or language, since everybody within the World Federation shares common criteria in terms of technique and forms.

I would also like to highlight the excellent work done by the athletes of the national team of Poomsae in Spain under the leadership of its technical director, D. José Santiago. Once again, they have proved their quality, showing in each technique, each position, each kick, the fruit of many years of hard training and learning. The result: A practical book and DVD, both for students who want to practice the Poomsae and for coaches and competitors who wish to update the latest movements, in the way they need to be performed for a perfect execution.

As I said in the previous presentation, "this is only the beginning". Our athletes and coaches are preparing what will be the official book of the courses for certification; later, we are thinking about making books and DVDs on High Competition, Hapkido and many other subjects of the rich and varied syllabus which forms the practice of Taekwondo at the highest level, such as exhibition, motivation, specific physical training for our sport, etc...

For all this, the Spanish Federation is pleased to offer all lovers of Taekwondo in over 50 countries and in six languages, its sincere and humble contribution to the expansion of this wonderful sport and Martial Art, with the certainty of having given the best of ourselves.

Jesús Castellanos
President of the Spanish Federation of Taekwondo

Preface

It is an honor for me to write a few lines as a presentation of this beautiful book and DVD on the High Poomsaes, made by *Budo International,* which meets an important need in the spreading and promotion of Taekwondo.

In the content of each poomsae in this book you can see the reflection of the unification of each technique in the world (WTF), based on the practical experience of each athlete, as the researcher aptitude of the technical team of the FET (Spanish Federation of Taekwondo).

Having read and studied it, it is noteworthy its value and contribution to the Philosophy of Taekwondo. Besides, this book intends to be a working tool, a text adapted to the needs of practitioners, coaches and managers, a partner that helps them to advance in the beautiful path of competition and teaching of Poomsaes.

The Spanish Federation of Taekwondo has undergone an amazing progression, as a result of many intense years of work, thanks to the efforts of all athletes, coaches, managers and our president, D. Jesús Castellanos.

D. Alfredo Tucci and his publishing house, *Budo International Publ. Co.,* deserve special mention in the task of getting this work to reach all fans, practitioners, coaches, managers and lovers of this beautiful martial art that is Taekwondo, especially the Poomsaes.

It is a work whose reading is fun, instructive and practical. It really shows the virtue of expressing the refinement of techniques through the tables and photos of our athletes, many of them champions of Spain, Europe and the World, all National team members of the FET, but avoiding to use repeating technicalities that could overwhelm any reader.

José Santiago Bueno
Technical Director of the Spanish Federation of Taekwondo

Introduction

This book that we present today brings together the highest forms, the most complex and rich of Taekwondo. Once the 8 first forms of Taekwondo have been mastered, the following ones are not only longer and more complex, but they include variations in angles and series of techniques at a more complex and intense level, leading the practitioner to a higher development of his technical work, coordination and organization.

The High Poomsae are certainly more aesthetically beautiful than their younger siblings, but the formers are the first and necessary step to reach this new frontier. This is the Marcial path; an upward path, where you must always be supported at the previous step to reach the next one.

After the success of the first part of this work, thanks to the publication of the book "Basic Poomsaes 1-8", it was essential to complete this project, according to the organization of the study of the forms established by the WTF (World Taekwondo Federation) for its members.

Even if nothing can replace a good Master, this book is the closest thing to the chance of learning under the guidance of the best names. For those who already know the forms, it is a way of remembering the sequences and reviewing the movements, with great world and European champions. It is certainly an excellent tool for all students, but especially for teachers, as it allows them to focus their work on correcting the pace, the sequencing of harmony of the movements and other essential details for which a Master is irreplaceable, avoiding the need to waste time in memorizing them.

Once again, it is the excellent Spanish team of Poomsaes and technique that performs these graceful forms for you step by step, complemented, for those who wish it, with a DVD, a form of study that will allow you to observe the performance. However, unlike the DVD, the book allows to review in any place, immediate access to the doubts, a quick and sequenced memorization without any equipment but just one thing: what a teacher of anatomy would call "the perfect clip", that is, the hands.

This publication has been directed by the president of the Spanish Federation of Taekwondo, D. Jesús Castellanos, and its technical director, D. José Santiago Bueno. Both of them have the most outstanding curriculum as practitioners, both have been Masters and teachers for many years, as well as excellent professionals of Taekwondo. I would like to thank both their hard work and dedication in this project, which marks a milestone in the spread of Taekwondo of the highest quality in six languages and in more than 54 countries, and also to all the participants in it. It has been a privilege to meet them personally, as they are true champions without doubt, both inside and outside the mat. From the youngest to the veterans, the people in this unique group have given the best of themselves for the realization of this project.

Alfredo Tucci
Director of Budo International

Antonio Moreno
Nerea Alamancos
Samuel Meilan
D. José Santiago
Josefina López

The Team in the Book

D. Jesús Castellanos

Pedro Campillo

Juan Miguel Gómez

Laura Kim

Curriculum Vitae for the two last years of the competitors, performers of Poomsaes in this book

Name:	Josefina López Pérez.
Date of Birth:	29-07-70
F.E.T. Black belt:	7th Dan.
W.T.F. Black belt:	3rd Dan.
Category:	Pair Male / Female 2 - Over 36 years old
Career highlights:	2006 Spain Championship, Pamplona (Navarra) Senior 2: 1st Gold medal. 2006 World Championship Seoul (Korea) Senior 2: 3rd Bronze medal. 2007 Spain Championship, Gandia, (Valencia) Senior 2: 1st Gold medal. 2007 World Championship Incheón, (Korea) Senior 2: 2nd Silver medal. Young 2, 1st Gold medal 2007 Europe Championship, Antalya, (Turkey) Senior 2: 1st Gold medal. Young 2: 1st Gold medal.

Name:	Pedro Campillo Frontera. Date of Birth: 27/03/1975
F.E.T Black belt:	5th Dan.
W.T.F Black belt:	3rd Dan.
Category:	Senior 2 male from 31 to 40 years old.
Career highlights:	2006 Spain Championship, Pamplona (Navarra) Senior 2: st Gold medal. 2006 World Championship, Seoul (Korea) Senior 2: 3rd Bronze medal. 2007 Spain Championship Gandia, (Valencia) Senior 2: 1st Gold medal. 2007 World Championship Incheon, (Korea) Senior 2: 2nd Silver medal. 2007 Europe Championship Antalya, (Turkey) Senior 2: 1st Gold medal. 2008 Spain Championship Alcobendas, (Madrid) Senior 2: 1st Gold medal.

Name:	Laura Kim Kim.
Date of Birth:	24-07-1982
F.E.T. Black belt:	4th Dan.
W.T.F Black belt:	4th Dan.
Category:	Senior 1 Women 19 to 30 years old.
Career highlights:	2006 Spain Championship Pamplona, (Navarra) Senior 1: 1st Gold medal. 2006 World Championship Seoul (Korea) Senior 1: 2nd Silver medal. 2007 Spain Championship Gandia, (Valencia) Senior 1: 1st Gold medal. 2007 World Championship Incheon, (Korea) Senior 1: $3r^{d}$ Bronze medal. 2007 Europe Championship Antalya, (Turkey) Senior 1: 1st Gold medal. 2008 Spain Championship Alcobendas, (Madrid) Senior 1: 1st Gold medal. Young 1: 1st Gold medal

Name:	Juan Miguel Gómez Gómez.
Date of Birth:	23-07-1991
F.E.T Black belt:	1st Dan.
W.T.F Black belt:	1st Dan.
Category:	Junior Men 14 to 18 years old.
Career highlights:	2007 Spain Championship Gandia, (Valencia) Junior: 1st Gold medal. 2007 World Championship Incheon, (Korea) Junior: 2nd Silver medal. 2007 Europe Championship Antalya, (Turkey) Junior 1: Gold medal. 2008 Spain Championship Alcobendas, (Madrid) Junior 1: Gold medal. Young, 1: 1st Gold medal

Name:	Samuel Meilen Fernández.
Date of birth:	31/01/1984
F.E.T Black belt:	4th Dan.
W.T.F Black belt:	2nd Dan.
Category:	Pair Male / Female 1 - from 14 to 35 years old.
Career highlights:	2007 Spain Championship Gandia, (Valencia), Pair 1: 1st Gold medal. 2007 World Championship Incheon, (Korea) Pair 1: $3r^{d}$ Bronze medal. 2007 Europe Championship Antalya, (Turkey) Pair 1: 2nd Silver medal.

Name:	Nerea Alamáncos Lamas.
Date of birth:	04/07/1987
F.E.T Black belt:	2nd Dan.
W.T.F Black belt:	1st Dan.
Category:	Pair Male / Female 1 - from 14 to 35 years old.
Career highlights:	2007 Spain Championship Gandia, (Valencia) Pair 1: 1st Gold medal. 2007 World Championship Incheon, (Korea) Pair 1: 3rd Bronze medal. 2007 Europe Championship Antalya, (Turkey) Pair 1: 2nd Silver medal.

Name:	Antonio Moreno Rodríguez.
Date of birth:	17-10-1970
F.E.T Black belt:	6th Dan.
W.T.F Black belt:	3rd Dan.
Category:	Pair Male / Female 2 - Over 36 years old.
Career highlights:	2007 Spain Championship Gandia, (Valencia) Pair 2: 1st Gold medal 2007 World Championship Incheon, (Korea) Pair 2: 1st Gold medal 2007 Europe Championship Antalya (Turkey) Pair 2: 1st Gold medal.

The High Poomsae are 9, and there is not a great difference in the hierarchy and difficulty of the forms (teguk).

9 POOMSAE KORYO

품세 고려

Koryo, symbolizes "seonbae"

士

The poomsae **Koryo** symbolizes "seonbae", the spirit of the brave people of the Koryo dynasty, who defended from the Mongol invaders. What represents a fair man is characterized by a strong martial spirit as well as a man with a fair spirit. The spirit has been inherited through the ages of Koguryo, Pahae and then Koryo, which is supported by the organization of poomsae Koryo, which can only be practiced by black belts. The jumbi-seogi is the tongmilgi, which requires mental concentration placing your hand between the low and high abdomen where "sin" (divinity) and "jeong" (spirit) converge. The line of poomsae represents the Chinese letter which means "seonbae" or "seonbi", a learned man or a virtuous man, in Korean language

10 POOMSAE KEUMGANG

품세 금강

Keumgang, symbolizes mountain

The movements of Pumse **Kumgang** are as beautiful as Kumgang-san (a Korean mountain) and as strong as Keumgang-seok (diamond), which has the meaning of toughness and meditation. The Keumgagn mountain, in the Korean peninsula, which is regarded as the center of the national spirit and the "Keumgang yoksa" (Keumgagn warrior), named after Buddha, who represents the powerful warrior, are the background to name this poomsae. The line of poomsae symbolizes a mountain shown by the Chinese letter. The movement should be powerful and well balanced to benefit / extol the dignity of black belts.

11 POOMSAE TAEBAEK

품세 태백

Taebaek, symbolizes lightness

The definition of **Taebaek** is "lightness". It represents the old name of the Paekdu mountain, where the legendary Tangun founded the Korean nation. Paekdu is a symbol for Korea, kingdom of the country, and the bright mountain symbolizes the sacred soul and thinking of Tangun of the "hongik ingan" (humanitarian ideal). There are many sites known as Taeback, but Paektu mountain, which has been typically known as the cradle of the Korean people, is the antecedent of the name of poomsae, Taeback. The line of poomsae is "klike", a Chinese letter, which symbolizes the bridge between Heaven and Earth, representing the man who founded the nation following an order from Heaven. Every move of this poomsae must not only be fast, but with determination and toughness.

12 POOMSAE PYONGWON

품세 평원

Pyongwon, symbolizes harmony

Pyongwon means "plain" and "harmony": great, majestic. It symbolizes the Earth and the basis for life and nature. It is the source of life for all creatures, the field where human beings live their lives. The poomsae Pyongwon was based on the idea of peace and fight resulting from the principles of origin and use. The line of poomsae means the origin and transformation of the plain.

13 POOMSAE SIPJIN

품세 십진

Sipjin, symbolizes the 10 longevities

The word **"Sipjin"** stands for 10 symbols of longevity. This thinking says that there are 10 creatures with long life: sun, moon, mountain, water, stone, pine tree, herb of eternal youth, turtle, deer and crane. It also means the infinite growth and development in a systematic order: stability. There are 2 celestial bodies, 3 natural sources, 2 plants and 3 animals, all representing the human being, hope and love. The poomsae Sipjin symbolizes those things. The Chinese letter which means 10 is shaped like the line of the poomsae, which means an infinite numbering of the decimal system and an unceasing development.

14 POOMSAE JITAE

품세 지태

Jitae, symbolizes Earth

The word **Jitae** derives from the meaning of the word "Earth". All things evolve, die and return to the earth, the earth is the beginning and the end of life. A man on earth represents how to fight for human life, such as kicks, jumps and footprints on the ground. Therefore, the poomsae symbolizes several aspects that occur during the fight for the existence of man. The line of poomsae means a man standing on earth to jump into the sky.

15 POOMSAE CHONKWON

품세 천권

Chonkwon, symbolizes Great powers of heaven

The word **"Chonkwon"** means great power from heaven. The sky should be seen as the ruler of the universe, which is the origin of all creatures and the cosmos itself. Since ancient times, man has looked at the sky as an infinite, mysterious, deep world. Its infinite competence means the creation, the complete change. Humans have used the name of Heaven for all forms and meanings on the earth, because they were frightened by the power of Heaven. More than 9,000 years ago, the founder of the Korean people, "Hwanin" was called the "heavenly king". He settled in the mountains, where the “Han” people, heavenly race, gave birth to the thinking and actions from which the Taekwondo came out. The poomsae Chonkwon is based on that sublime history and on those thoughts. The movements of Cheonkwon are full of piety and vitality.

16 POOMSAE HANSU

품세 한수

Hansu, symbolizes water

The word **"Hansu"** means "Water"; fluidity and adaptability are expressed in the nature of water, which is the source of the substance that preserves the life and growth of all creatures. Hansu symbolizes the birth of a life and growth, strength and weakness, magnanimity and harmony, and adaptability. Especially, "Han" has several meanings, mainly the name of a country, variety, nobility, equality, length and even the sky and the roof of everything.

17 POOMSAE ILYO

품세 일여

Ilyo, symbolizes one, unity of mind and body

卍

The state of spiritual cultivation in Buddhism is called **"Ilyo"**, which means the thinking of the great Buddhist father of the Silla dynasty, San Wonhyo, who is characterized by the philosophy of the unity of mind (spirit) and body (material). It teaches that one point, a line or a circle finish after rolling into one. That is why the poomsae Ileo represents the harmonization of spirit and body, which is the highest ideal of Taekwondo which can be found in this state, the essence of martial arts. It is a discipline in which we concentrate on every move, leaving all the materialistic thoughts, obsessions and external influences behind. It means that the mind and body are one; unity, after a long training and various types of spiritual cultivation and techniques to complete the practice of Taekwondo. The line of poomsae symbolizes the Buddhist sign (swastika), in memory of San Wonho, that means a state of perfect self in Buddhism where the origin, substance and service are congruent.

KIBON HYONG
Essential vocabulary

AHOB: . . . . Nine.
AKUNSON: . . . . Hand arch.
AN PALMOK: . . . . Inside part of the forearm.
AN: . . . . inwards.
AP CHUK: . . . . Foot metatarsus.
AP OLLIGUI: . . . . Frontal leg lifting.
AP: . . . . To the front.
ARE: . . . . Down (from the waist down).
BAKAT: . . . . Outwards.
BAL: . . . . Foot.
BALBADAK: . . . . Foot sole.
BALDUNG: . . . . Foot instep.
BALNAL: . . . . Outside of the foot.
BARO: . . . . Go back to the initial position.
BATANG SON: . . . . Palm.
BE: . . . . Abdomen.
BEGIN: . . . . Tie.
BESING: . . . . Supreme.
BITURO: . . . . Twist.
CHAGUI: . . . . Kick.
CHAKUNDOL CHOGUI: . . . . Small hinge.
CHARIOT: . . . . Standing, greeting position.
CHECHO: . . . . Fist upwards.
CHI: . . . . Upwards.
CHIGUI: . . . . Blow.
CHIL: . . . . Seventh.
CHIRUGUI: . . . . Prick.
CHOCHIN: . . . . Move forward.
CHONCHIN: . . . . Forward.
CHONG: . . . . Blue.
CHUMBI: . . . . Warm-up position.
CHUMOK: . . . . Fist.
CHUNGAL: . . . . Tibia.
DANGKIOK: . . . . Grab.
DARI: . . . . Leg.

DASOT: .... Five.
DO: .... Path.
DOBOK: .... Taekwondo uniform.
DOCHANG: .... Training room.
DOLLYO: .... Circular.
DUBONG: .... Double.
DUL: .... Two.
DUNG: .... Back.
FUCHIN: .... Backwards.
GAWY: .... Scissors.
GECHIO: .... Cross back.
GODURO: .... One hand goes with the other hand.
GONGKIOK: .... Attack.
GU: .... Ninth.
GUMAN: .... Final.
HANA: .... One.
HONG: .... Red.
I: .... Second.
IL: .... First.
ILGOB: .... Seven.
JIRUGUI: .... Fist attack.
KALYO: .... Stop.
KAMCHOM: .... -1 point less.
KESOK: .... Continue.
KIAP: .... Shout.
KIBON KISUL: .... Essential technique.
KIONÑE: .... Greeting.
KISUL: .... Technique.
KUKIE: .... Flag
KUMAN: .... Finish.
MAGKI: .... Defense.
ME CHUMOK: .... Fist base.
MOK: .... Neck.
MOM: .... Body.
MON DOLLIO: .... Turn.
MONTONG: .... Middle.
MORI: .... Head.
MUGOL: .... Side.
MURUP: .... Knee.

NET: . . . . Fourth.
O: . . . . Fifth.
OLGUL: . . . . Upwards.
OLIGUI: . . . . Lifting.
OLLYO: . . . . Upwards.
ORUM: . . . . Right.
PAL: . . . . Eighth.
PALKUP: . . . . Elbow.
PALMOK: . . . . Wrist.
PUM: . . . . Special movement.
PUMSE: . . . . Ideogram of technical movements.
SA: . . . . Fourth.
SABOMNIN: . . . . Master.
SAM: . . . . Third.
SEO: . . . . Pause.
SET: . . . . Three.
SIGAN: . . . . Time.
SIO: . . . . Pause.
SIP: . . . . Tenth.
SIYAK: . . . . Start.
SOGUI: . . . . Position.
SON KUT: . . . . Hand point.
SON: . . . . Hand.
SUN: . . . . Winner.
GUKI: . . . . Flag.
TI: . . . . Belt.
TOK: . . . . Chin.
TUI DORA: . . . . Turn on the back.
TUIO: . . . . Jump.
TUIT: . . . . Backwards.
WEN: . . . . Left.
YEOL: . . . . Ten.
YODOUL: . . . . Eight.
YOL: . . . . Ten.
YOP: . . . . Lateral.
YOSOT: . . . . Six.
YU SHIM: . . . . Referee.
YUCK: . . . . Sixth.

TAEKWONDO

9 POOMSAE KORYO

"SEONBAE"

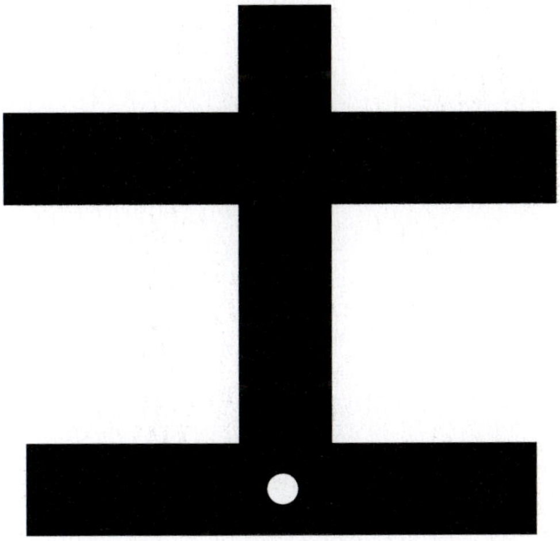

품세

고려

Chariot

Naranji Sogui
Tong Milgui
Chunbi

Orun
Tuit Kubi
Sonnal
Momtong
Makki

Orun Bal
Yop Chagui
Are

Orun Bal
Yop Chagui
Momtong

Orun
Ap Kubi
Sonnal
Bakkat
Chigui

Orun
Ap Kubi
Momtong
Baro Jirugui

Wen
Tuit Kubi
Momtong
Makki

Wen
Tuit Kubi
Sonnal
Momtong
Makki

Wen Bal
Yop Chagui
Are

Wen Bal
Yop Chagui
Momtong

Wen
Ap Kubi
Sonnal
Bakkat
Chigui

Wen
Ap Kubi
Momtong
Baro Jirugui

Orun
Tuit Kubi
Momtong
Makki

Wen
Ap Kubi
Hansonnal
Are Makki

Wen
Ap Kubi
Agumson
Kalchebi

Orun Bal
Ap Chagui

Orun
Ap Kubi
Hansonnal
Are Makki

Orun
Ap Kubi
Agumson
Kalchebi

Wen Bal
Ap Chagui

Wen
Ap Kubi
Hansonnal
Are Makki

Wen Ap Kubi
Agumson Kalchebi (Kihap)

Orun Bal
Ap Chagui

Orun Ap Kubi
Murup Koki

Orun
Ap Kubi
An Palmok
Momtong
Gechio
Makki

Wen Bal
Ap Chagui

Wen
Ap Kubi
Murup
Koki

Wen Ap Sogui An Palmok Momtong Gechio Makki

Chuchum Sogui Hansonnal Momtong Yop Makki

Chuchum Sogui Piochok Jirugui

Orun
Ap Koa
Sogui
Piochok
Jirugui

Wen Bal
Yop Chagui
Chagun Dol
Chogui

Orun
Ap Kubi
Dangkio Are
Pyonson Kut
Checho
Chirugui

Orun
Ap Sogui
Are Makki

Wen
Ap Sogui
Batangson
Nulo Makki

Chuchum
Sogui
Palkup Yop
Chigui

Orun
Chuchum
Sogui
Hansonnal
Momtong
Yop Makki

Orun
Chuchum
Sogui
Piochok
Jirugui

Wen
Ap Koa
Sogui
Piochok
Jirugui

Orun Bal
Yop Chagui
Chagun Dol
Chogui

Wen
Ap Kubi
Dangkio Are
Pyonson Kut
Checho
Chirugui

Wen
Ap Sogui
Are Makki

Orun
Ap Sogui
Batangson
Nulo Makki

Chuchum
Sogui
Palkup Yop
Chigui

Moa Sogui
Me Chumok
Are Piochok
Chigui

Wen
Ap Kubi
Sonnal
Bakkat
Chigui

Wen
Ap Kubi
Hansonnal
Are Makki

Orun
Ap Kubi
Sonnal
Mok Chigui

Orun
Ap Kubi
Hansonnal
Are Makki

Orun
Ap Kubi
Sonnal
Mok
Chigui

Wen
Ap Kubi
Hansonnal
Are Makki

Orun
Ap Kubi
Agumson
Kalchebi
(Kihap)

Naranji
Sogui
Tong Milgui
Chunbi

Chariot

Daedo

10 POOMSAE KEUMGANG

• MOUNTAIN • MONTAÑA
• BERG • MONTAGNA • MONTAGNE

품세

금강

Chariot

Chunbi

Wen
Ap Kubi
An Palmok
Momtong
Gechio
Makki

Orun
Ap Kubi
Batangson
Tok Chigui

Wen
Ap Kubi
Batangson
Tok Chigui

Orun
Ap Kubi
Batangson
Tok Chigui

Orun
Tuit Kubi
Hansonnal
Momtong
Makki

Wen
Tuit Kubi
Hansonnal
Momtong
Makki

Orun
Tuit Kubi
Hansonnal
Momtong
Makki

• Preparation of the technical number 8
• Preparación de la técnica número 8
• Vorbereitung technischer Nr. 8
• Preparazione del numero tecnico 8
• Préparation du nombre technique 8

8

Orun Bal Jakdari Sogui Kumgang Makki

9

Chuchum Sogui Kun Dol Chogui

• Preparation of the technical number 10
• Preparación de la técnica número 10
• Vorbereitung technischer Nr. 10
• Preparazione del numero tecnico 10
• Préparation du nombre technique 10

Chuchum Sogui Kun Dol Chogui

Chuchum Sogui Santul Makki (Kihap)

Chuchum
Sogui
An Palmok
Momtong
Gechio
Makki

Naranji
Sogui
Are
Gechio
Makki

Chuchum
Sogui
Santul
Makki

• Preparation of the technical number 15
• Preparación de la técnica número 15
• Vorbereitung technischer Nr. 15
• Preparazione del numero tecnico 15
• Préparation du nombre technique 15

15

Wem Bal Jakdari Sogui Kumgang Makki

16

Chuchum Sogui Kun Dol Chogui

- **Preparation of the technical number 17**
- **Preparación de la técnica número 17**
- **Vorbereitung technischer Nr. 17**
- **Preparazione del numero tecnico 17**
- **Préparation du nombre technique 17**

Chuchum Sogui Kun Dol Chogui

- **Preparation of the technical number 18**
- **Preparación de la técnica número 18**
- **Vorbereitung technischer Nr. 18**
- **Preparazione del numero tecnico 18**
- **Préparation du nombre technique 18**

Wen Bal Jakdari Sogui
Kumgang Makki

Chuchum Sogui
Kun Dol Chogui

- **Preparation of the technical number 20**
- **Preparación de la técnica número 20**
- **Vorbereitung technischer Nr. 20**
- **Preparazione del numero tecnico 20**
- **Préparation du nombre technique 20**

Chuchum Sogui Kun Dol Chogui

Chuchum Sogui Santul Makki (Kihap)

Chuchum Sogui An Palmok Momtong Gechio Makki

Naranji
Sogui
Are
Gechio
Makki

Chuchum
Sogui
Santul
Makki

- Preparation of the technical number 25
- Preparación de la técnica número 25
- Vorbereitung technischer Nr. 25
- Preparazione del numero tecnico 25
- Préparation du nombre technique 25

Orun Bal Jakdari Sogui
Kumgang Makki

Chuchum Sogui
Kun Dol Chogui

- Preparation of the technical number 27
- Preparación de la técnica número 27
- Vorbereitung technischer Nr. 27
- Preparazione del numero tecnico 27
- Préparation du nombre technique 27

Chuchum Sogui
Kun Dol Chogui

Chunbi

Chariot

11 POOMSAE TAEBEK

• LIGHTNESS • LIGERESA
• LEICHTIGKEIT • LEGGEREZZA • LÉGÈRETÉ

품세

태백

Chariot

Chunbi

Wen
Bom Sogui
Sonnal
Are Gechio
Makki

Orun Bal
Ap Chagui

Orun
Ap Kubi
Momtong
Dubong
Jirugui

Orun
Ap Kubi
Momtong
Dubong
Jirugui

Orun
Bom Sogui
Sonnal
Are Gechio
Makki

Wen Bal
Ap Chagui

Wen
Ap Kubi
Momtong
Dubong
Jirugui

Wen
Ap Kubi
Momtong
Dubong
Jirugui

Wen
Ap Kubi
Chebipum
Mok Chigui

Orun
Ap Kubi
Kolcho
Makki

6.1

Orun
Ap Kubi
Momtong
Baro Jirugui

7

Wen
Ap Kubi
Kolcho
Makki

7.1

Wen
Ap Kubi
Momtong
Baro Jirugui

Orun
Ap Kubi
Kolcho
Makki

Orun
Ap Kubi
Momtong
Baro Jirugui
(Kihap)

- **Preparation of the technical number 9**
- **Preparación de la técnica número 9**
- **Vorbereitung technischer Nr. 9**
- **Preparazione del numero tecnico 9**
- **Préparation du nombre technique 9**

Orun
Tuit Kubi
Keumgang
Momtong
Makki

Orun
Tuit Kubi
Dangkio
Tok Jirugui

Orun
Tuit Kubi
Momtong
Jirugui

Orun Bal Jakdari Sogui
Chagun Dol Chogui

Wen Bal
Yop chagui

Wen Ap Kubi
Momtong Palkup Piochok Chuigui

Moa Sogui

- Preparation of the technical number 14
- Preparación de la técnica número 14
- Vorbereitung technischer Nr. 14
- Preparazione del numero tecnico 14
- Préparation du nombre technique 14

14

Wen Tuit Kubi Keumgang Momtong Makki

15

Wen Tuit Kubi Dangkio Tok Jirugui

Wen
Tuit Kubi
Momtong
Jirugui

Wen Bal
Jakdari
Sogui
Chagun Dol
Chogui

Orun Bal
Yop chagui

Orun
Ap Kubi
Momtong
Palkup
Piochok
Chuigui

Moa Sogui

- Preparation of the technical number 19
- Preparación de la técnica número 19
- Vorbereitung technischer Nr. 19
- Preparazione del numero tecnico 19
- Préparation du nombre technique 19

Orun
Tuit Kubi
Sonnal
Momtong
Makki

Orun
Ap Kubi
Pyonson Kut
Seuo
Chirugui

Wen
Ap Kubi
Chapin
Sonmok
Mitro Pegui

Orun
Tuit Kubi
Dung
Chumok
Bakkat
Chigui

Orun
Ap Kubi
Momtong
Bande
Jirugui
(Kihap)

Wen
Ap Kubi
Gawi Makki

Orun Bal
Ap Chagui

Orun
Ap Kubi
Momtong
Dubong
Jirugui

Orun
Ap Kubi
Momtong
Dubong
Jirugui

Orun
Ap Kubi
Gawi Makki

Wen Bal
Ap Chagui

Wen
Ap Kubi
Momtong
Dubong
Jirugui

Wen
Ap Kubi
Momtong
Dubong
Jirugui

Chunbi

Chariot

TAE KWON DO
Dae do

12 POOMSAE PYONGWON

• HARMONY • ARMONIA
• HARMONIE • ARMONIA • HARMONIE

품세

평원

Chariot

Chunbi
Moa Sogui
Kiopson
Chunbi
Sogui

Wen
Naranji
Sogui
Sonnal
Are Gechio
Makki

Wen
Naranji
Sogui
Tong Milgui
Chunbi

Wen
Tuit Kubi
Hansonnal
Are Makki

Orun
Tuit Kubi
Hansonnal
Momtong
Bakkat
Makki

Wen
Ap Kubi
Palkup
Ollyo Chigui

Orun Bal
Ap Chagui

Wen Bal
Yop Chagui

6.2

Wen
Tuit Kubi
Sonnal
Momtong
Makki

7

Wen
Tuit Kubi
Sonnal
Are Makki

8

Chuchum
Sogui
Goduro
Olgul Yop
Makki

• Preparation of the technical number 9
• Preparación de la técnica número 9
• Vorbereitung technischer Nr. 9
• Preparazione del numero tecnico 9
• Préparation du nombre technique 9

Chuchum Sogui Dung Chumok Dangkio Tok Chigui

Chuchum Sogui Dung Dangkio Chumok Tok Chigui

Wen
Ap Koa
Sogui
Mohe
Chigui

Chuchum
Sogui
Gechio
Santul
Maki

Wen Bal
Jakdari
Sogui
Keumgang
Makki

Wen Bal Jakdari Sogui
Chagun Dol Chogui

Orun Bal
Yop Chagui

Orun Ap Kubi
Palkup Ollyo Chigui

Wen Bal
Ap Chagui

Orun Bal
Yop Chagui

Orun
Tuit Kubi
Sonnal
Momtong
Makki

Orun
Tuit Kubi
Sonnal
Are Makki

Chuchum
Sogui
Goduro
Olgul Yop
Makki

- **Preparation of the technical number 17**
- **Preparación de la técnica número 17**
- **Vorbereitung technischer Nr. 17**
- **Preparazione del numero tecnico 17**
- **Préparation du nombre technique 17**

Chuchum Sogui Dung Chumok Dangkio Top Chigui

Chuchum Sogui Dung Chumok Dangkio Top Chigui

Orun Ap Koa Sogui Mohe Chigui

Chuchum
Sogui
Gechio
Santul
Maki

Orun Bal
Jakdari
Sogui
Keumgang
Makki

Orun Bal
Jakdari
Sogui
Chagun Dol
Chogui

21

Wen Bal
Yop Chagui

21.1

Wen
Ap Kubi
Momtong
Palkup
Piochok
Chigui

Moa Sogui
Kiopson
Chunbi
Sogui

Chariot

PEDRO CAMPILLO
Daedo

13 POOMSAE SIPJIN

- 10 SYMBOLS OF LONGEVITY
- 10 LONGEVIDADES
- DIE 10 LEBENSLÄNGEN
- 10 LONGEVITÀ
- LES 10 LONGÉVITÉS

품세 십진

Chariot

Chunbi

Naranji
Sogui
Wangso
Maki

Naranji
Sogui
Wangso
Maki

Orun
Tuit Kubi
Sonbadak
Goduro
Momtong
Bakkat
Makki

Wen
Ap Kubi
Pyoson Kut
Opo Chirugui

Wen
Ap Kubi
Momtong
Dubong
Jirugui

Wen
Ap Kubi
Momtong
Dubong
Jirugui

Chuchum
Sogui
Gechio
Santul
Makki

Wen
Ap Koa
Sogui

Chuchum
Sogui
Yop Jirugui
(Kihap)

Chuchum
Sogui
Mohe Chigui

Wen
Tuit Kubi
Sonbadak
Goduro
Momtong
Bakkat
Makki

Orun
Ap Kubi
Pyoson Kut
Opo Chirugui

Orun
Ab Kubi
Momtong
Dubong
Jirugui

Orun
Ab Kubi
Momtong
Dubong
Jirugui

Chuchum
Sogui
Gechio
Santul
Makki

Orun
Ap Koa
Sogui

Chuchum
Sogui
Yop Jirugui
(Kihap)

Chuchum
Sogui
Mohe Chigui

Wen
Tuit Kubi
Sonbadak
Goduro
Momtong
Bakkat
Makki

Orun
Ap Kubi
Pyoson Kut
Opo Chirugui

Orun
Ab Kubi
Momtong
Dubong
Jirugui

Orun
Ab Kubi
Momtong
Dubong
Jirugui

Orun
Tuip Kubi
Sonnal
Are Makki

Orun
Ap Kubi
Bawi Milgui

Chuchum
Sogui
Sonnal Dung
Gechio
Momtong
Makki

Chuchum
Sogui
Sonnal
Gechio
Are Makki

Gechio
Are Makki

Wen
Ap Kubi
Gorro
Olligui

Wen
Ap Kubi
Bawi Milgui

Orun Bal
Ap Chagui

Orun
Ap Kubi
Chetdari
Jirugui

Wen Bal
Ap Chagui

Wen
Ap Kubi
Chetdari
Jirugui

Orun Bal
Ap Chagui

Wen
Tuit Koa
Sogui
Dung
Chumok
Goduro
Olgul
Ape Chigui
(Kihap)

Wen
Ap Kubi
Bawi Milgui

Wen
Bom Sogui
Sonnal
Okgoro
Are Makki

Wen
Tuit Kubi
Sonnal Dung
Montong
Makki

Orun
Tuit Kubi
Chetdari
Jirugui

Wen
Tuit Kubi
Chetdari
Jirugui

Chunbi

Chariot

14 POOMSAE JITAE

• EARTH • TIERRA
• ERDE • TERRA • TERRE

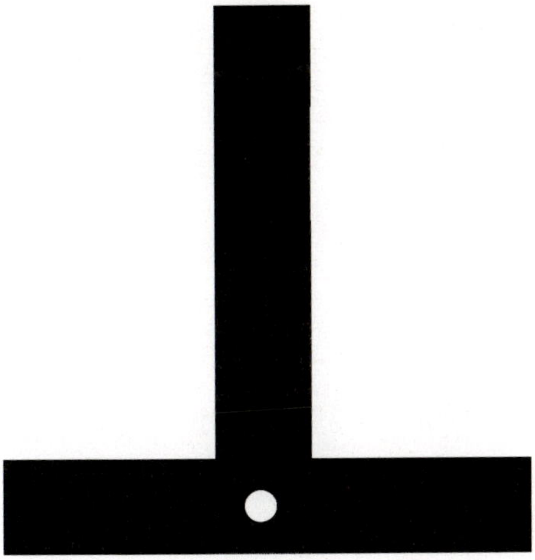

품세 지태

Chariot

Chunbi

Orun
Tuit Kubi
An Palmok
Momtong
Bakkat
Makki

Orun
Ap Kubi
Olgul Makki

Orun
Ap Kubi
Momtong
Baro Jirugui

Wen
Tuit Kubi
An Palmok
Momtong
Bakkat
Makki

Wen
Ap Kubi
Olgul Makki

Wen
Ap Kubi
Momtong
Baro Jirugui

Wen
Ap Kubi
Are Makki

Orun
Tuit Kubi
Hansonnal
Olgul Makki

Orun Bal
Ap Chagui

Wen
Tuit Kubi
Sonnal
Are Makki

Wen
Tuit Kubi
Momtong
Bakkat
Makki

Wen Bal
Ap Chagui

Orun
Tuit Kubi
Sonnal
Are Makki

Wen
Ap Kubi
Olgul Makki

Orun
Ap Kubi
Keumgang
Ap Jirugui

Orun
Ap Kubi
Momtong
An Makki

Orun
Ap Kubi
Goduro
Momtong
Makki

Wen
Tuit Kubi
Hansonnal
Are Makki

Orun Bal
Ap Chagui

Wen
Ap Kubi
Momtong
Dubong
Jirugui

Wen
Ap Kubi
Momtong
Dubong
Jirugui

Chuchum
Sogui
Wangso
Makki

Chuchum Sogui Are Yop Makki

Chuchum Sogui Jansonnal Momtong Yop Makki

Chuchum Sogui Me Chumok Piochok Chigui (Kihap)

Wen Bal
Jakdari
Sogui
Are Yop
Makki

Wen Bal
Jakdari
Sogui
Chagun
Dol Chogui

Orun Bal
Yop Chagui

Orun Bal Jakdari Sogui
Yop Are Makki

Orun Bal Jakdari Sogui
Chagun Dol Chogui

Wen Bal
Yop Chagui

Wen
Ap Kubi
Momtong
Baro Jirugui

Orun
Ap Kubi
Momtong
Bande
Jirugui
(Kihap)

Orun
Tuit Kubi
Sonnal
Are Makki

Wen
Tuit Kubi
Sonnal
Momtong
Makki

Wen
Tuit Kubi
Sonnal
Are Makki

Orun
Tuit Kubi
Sonnal
Momtong
Makki

Chunbi

Chariot

15 POOMSAE CHONKWON

- GREAT POWER FROM HEAVEN
- GRAN PODER DEL CIELO
- DIE GROSSE MACHT DES HIMMELS
- GRANDE POTERE DEL CIELO
- GRAND POUVOIR DU CIEL

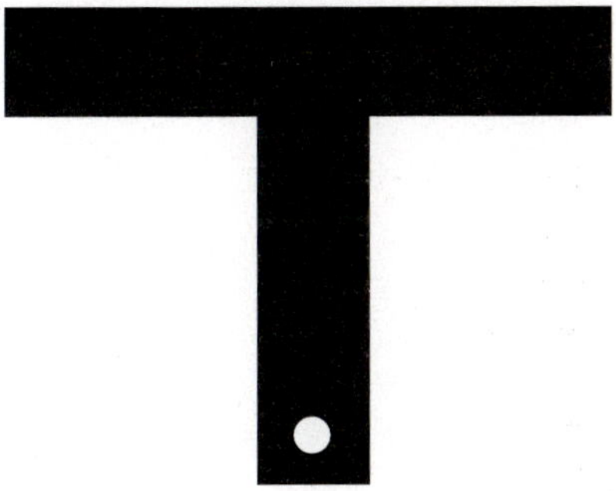

품세

천권

Chariot

Moa Sogui
Kiopson
Chunbi
Sogui

Moa Sogui
Nalgue
Piogui

Orun
Bom Sogui
Bam Chumok
Sosum Chigui

Orun
Ap Kubi
Bituro
Hansonnal
Momtong
Bakkat
Makki

- **Preparation of the technical number 4**
- **Preparación de la técnica número 4**
- **Vorbereitung technischer Nr. 4**
- **Preparazione del numero tecnico 4**
- **Préparation du nombre technique 4**

Wen
Ap Kubi
Momtong
Baro Jirugui

Wen
Ap Kubi
Bituro
Hansonnal
Momtong
Bakkat
Makki

- Preparation of the technical number 6
- Preparación de la técnica número 6
- Vorbereitung technischer Nr. 6
- Preparazione del numero tecnico 6
- Préparation du nombre technique 6

Orun
Ap Kubi
Momtong
Baro Jirugui

Orun
Ap Kubi
Bituro
Hansonnal
Momtong
Bakkat
Makki

- **Preparation of the technical number 8**
- **Preparación de la técnica número 8**
- **Vorbereitung technischer Nr. 8**
- **Preparazione del numero tecnico 8**
- **Préparation du nombre technique 8**

Wen Bal
Yop Chagui
(Kihap)

Wen
Ap Kubi
Are Makki

Orun
Ap Kubi
Momtong
Bande
Jirugui

Orun
Tuit Kubi
An Palmok
Goduro
Momtong
Bakkat
Makki

Orun
Tuib Kubi
Momtong
Jirugui

- **Preparation of the technical number 12**
- **Preparación de la técnica número 12**
- **Vorbereitung technischer Nr. 12**
- **Preparazione del numero tecnico 12**
- **Préparation du nombre technique 12**

Wen
Tuit Kubi
Momtong
Jirugui

Wen
Tuit Kubi
An Palmok
Goduro
Momtong
Bakkat
Makki

Wen
Tuit Kubi
Momtong
Jirugui

• Preparation of the technical number 15
• Preparación de la técnica número 15
• Vorbereitung technischer Nr. 15
• Preparazione del numero tecnico 15
• Préparation du nombre technique 15

15

Orun Tuit Kubi Momtong Jirugui

16

16

Wen Ap Kubi An Palmok Bituro Momtong Bakkat Makki

Wen
Ap Kubi
Momtong
Bande
Jirugui

Orun Bal
Ap Chagui

Orun
Ap Kubi
Momtong
Bande
Jirugui

Wen
Tuit Kubi
Sonnal
Are Makki

Wen
Tuit Kubi
An Palmok
Momtong
Bakkat
Makki

Wen
Tuit Kubi
Goduro
Are Makki

21

21

Chuchum Sogui Keumgang Yop Jirugui

- Preparation of the technical number 22
- Preparación de la técnica número 22
- Vorbereitung technischer Nr. 22
- Preparazione del numero tecnico 22
- Préparation du nombre technique 22

22

22

Orun Bal Tuio Mom Dollyo Piochok Chagui

22.1

22.1

Chuchum Sogui Keumgang Yop Jirugui

Orun
Tuit Kubi
Sonnal
Oe Santul
Makki

Wen
Tuit Kubi
Sonnal
Oe Santul
Makki

Moa Sogui

- Preparation of the technical number 25
- Preparación de la técnica número 25
- Vorbereitung technischer Nr. 25
- Preparazione del numero tecnico 25
- Préparation du nombre technique 25

Moa Sogui
• Preparation of the technical number 25
• Preparación de la técnica número 25
• Vorbereitung technischer Nr. 25
• Preparazione del numero tecnico 25
• Préparation du nombre technique 25

Moa Sogui
• Preparation of the technical number 25
• Preparación de la técnica número 25
• Vorbereitung technischer Nr. 25
• Preparazione del numero tecnico 25
• Préparation du nombre technique 25

Orun Bom Sogui Taesan Milgui

Moa Sogui
- Preparation of the technical number 26
- Preparación de la técnica número 26
- Vorbereitung technischer Nr. 26
- Preparazione del numero tecnico 26
- Préparation du nombre technique 26

Moa Sogui
- Preparation of the technical number 26
- Preparación de la técnica número 26
- Vorbereitung technischer Nr. 26
- Preparazione del numero tecnico 26
- Préparation du nombre technique 26

Moa Sogui
- Preparation of the technical number 26
- Preparación de la técnica número 26
- Vorbereitung technischer Nr. 26
- Preparazione del numero tecnico 26
- Préparation du nombre technique 26

Wen
Bom Sogui
Taesan
Milgui

Moa Sogui
Kiopson
Chunbi
Sogui

Chariot

JOSEFINA

16 POOMSAE JANSU

• WATER • AGUA
• WASSER • ACQUA • EAU

품세 한수

Chariot

Moa Sogui
Kiopson
Chunbi

Wen
Ap Kubi
Sonnal
Dung
Gechio
Momtong
Makki

Orun
Ap Kubi
Du Me
Chumok
Yang
Yopguri
Chigui

Orun
Ap Kubi
Oe Santul
Makki

Wen
Ap Kubi
Momtong
Baro
Jirugui

5

Wen
Ap Kubi
Oe Santul
Makki

6

Orun
Ap Kubi
Momtong
Baro
Jirugui

7

Orun
Ap Kubi
Oe Santul
Makki

Wen
Ap Kubi
Momtong
Baro
Jirugui

Orun
Ap Kubi
Sonnal
Dung
Gechio
Momtong
Makki

- Preparation of the technical number 10
- Preparación de la técnica número 10
- Vorbereitung technischer Nr. 10
- Preparazione del numero tecnico 10
- Préparation du nombre technique 10

10

Wen
Ap Kubi
Agumson
Kalchebi

11

Orun
Kiotari
Sogui
Du Checho
Jirugui

12

Chuchum
Sogui
An Palmok
Are Piochok
Makki

Orun Tuit Kubi
Sonnal Keumgang Are Makki

Orun Bal Jakdari Sogui
Chagun Dol Chogui

Wen Bal
Yop Chagui

Wen
Ap Kubi
Chebipum
Mok Chigui

Orun Bal
Ap Chagui

Wen
Tuit Koa
Sogui
Dung
Chumok
Ape Chigui
(Kihap)

Chuchum Sogui Sonnal Bakkat Chigui

Orun Bal Piochok Chagui

Chuchum Sogui Momtong Piochok Palkup Chigui

• Preparation of the technical number 19
• Preparación de la técnica número 19
• Vorbereitung technischer Nr. 19
• Preparazione del numero tecnico 19
• Préparation du nombre technique 19

Orun Ap Kubi Agumson Kalchebi

Wen Kiotari Sogui Du Checho Jirugui

Chuchum Sogui
An Palmok Are Piochok Makki

Wen Tuit Kubi
Sonnal Keumgang Are Makki

Wen Bal Jakdari Sogui
Chagun Dol Chogui

Orun Bal
Yop Chagui

Orun
Ap Kubi
Chebipum
Mok Chigui

Wen Bal
Ap Chagui

Orun Tuit Koa Sogui Dung Chumok Ape Chigui (Kihap)

Chuchum Sogui Sonnal Bakkat Chigui

Wen Bal Piochok Chagui

Chuchum Sogui Momtong Piochok Palkup Chigui

Moa Sogui Kiopson Chunbi Sogui

Chariot

17 POOMSAE ILYO

- ONE, UNITY OF MIND AND BODY
- UNO, UNIDAD MENTE Y CUERPO
- DIE EINHEIT DES GEISTES UND DES KÖRPERS
- UNO, UNITÀ DI MENTE E CORPO
- UN, UNITÉ CORPS-ESPRIT

卍

품세 일여

ESPAÑA
ESP

Chariot

Moa Sogui
Bo Chumok
Chunbi

Orun
Tuit Kubi
Sonnal
Momtong
Makki

Orun
Ap Kubi
Momtong
Bande
Jirugui

Orun
Tuit Kubi
Keumgang
Maki

Orun
Tuit Kubi
Sonnal
Momtong
Makki

Orun Tuit Kubi Momtong Baro Jirugui

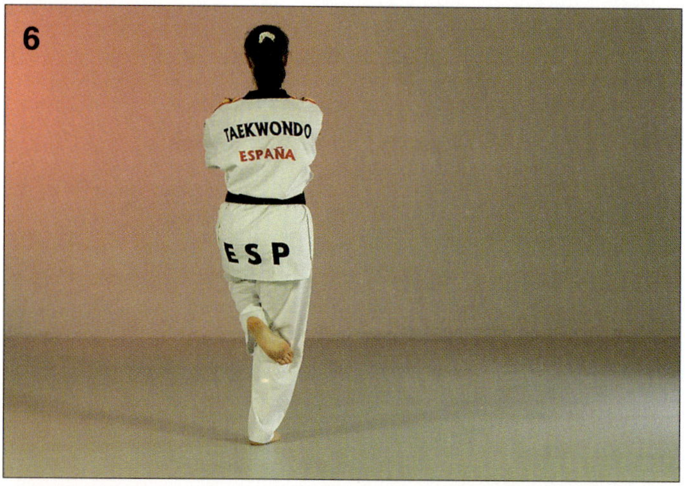

Orun Bal Ogun Sogui Goduro Piosong Kut Seuo Chirugui (Kihap)

- Preparation of the technical number 7
- Preparación de la técnica número 7
- Vorbereitung technischer Nr. 7
- Preparazione del numero tecnico 7
- Préparation du nombre technique 7

Wen Bal
Oe Santul
Yop Chagui

Orun
Tuit Kubi
Okgoro
Olgul Makki

- Preparation of the technical number 9
- Preparación de la técnica número 9
- Vorbereitung technischer Nr. 9
- Preparazione del numero tecnico 9
- Préparation du nombre technique 9

Orun
Ap Kubi
Momtong
Bande
Jirugui

Orun
Tuit Kubi
Kungang
Makki

Orun
Tuit Kubi
Sonnal
Momtong
Makki

Orun
Tuit Kubi
Momtong
Baro
Jirugui

Orun Bal
Ogun Sogui
Goduro
Piosong Kut
Seuo
Chirugui
(Kihap)

- Preparation of the technical number 14
- Preparación de la técnica número 14
- Vorbereitung technischer Nr. 14
- Preparazione del numero tecnico 14
- Préparation du nombre technique 14

14

Wen Bal
Oe Santul
Yop Chagui

15

Orun
Tuit Kubi
Okgoro
Olgul Makki

- Preparation of the technical number 16
- Preparación de la técnica número 16
- Vorbereitung technischer Nr. 16
- Preparazione del numero tecnico 16
- Préparation du nombre technique 16

16

Orun
Ap Kubi
Momtong
Bande
Jirugui

17

Orun
Tuit Kubi
Kungang
Maki

- **Preparation of the technical number 18**
- **Preparación de la técnica número 18**
- **Vorbereitung technischer Nr. 18**
- **Preparazione del numero tecnico 18**
- **Préparation du nombre technique 18**

Moa Sogui
Du Chumok
Jori Chunbi

Orun Bal
Ap Chagui

Wen Bal
Tuio
Yop Chagui

Orun
Tuit Kubi
Okgoro
Olgul Makki

- Preparation of the technical number 20
- Preparación de la técnica número 20
- Vorbereitung technischer Nr. 20
- Preparazione del numero tecnico 20
- Préparation du nombre technique 20

Orun
Ap Kubi
Momtong
Bande
Jirugui

Orun
Tuit Kubi
Kungang
Maki

- Preparation of the technical number 22
- Preparación de la técnica número 22
- Vorbereitung technischer Nr. 22
- Preparazione del numero tecnico 22
- Préparation du nombre technique 22

Moa Sogui
Du Chumok
Jori Chunbi

Wen Bal
Ap Chagui

Orun Bal
Yop Chagui

Wen
Tuit Kubi
Okgoro
Olgul Makki

- **Preparation of Bo Chumok Chunbi**
- **Preparación del final Bo Chumok Chunbi**
- **Vorbereitung Bo Chumok Chunbi**
- **Preparazione Bo Chumok Chunbi**
- **Préparation de la finale Bo Chumok Chunbi**

Moa Sogui Bo Chumok Chunbi

Chariot